From Micaela
6th Nov 200

Then & Now
Scarborough

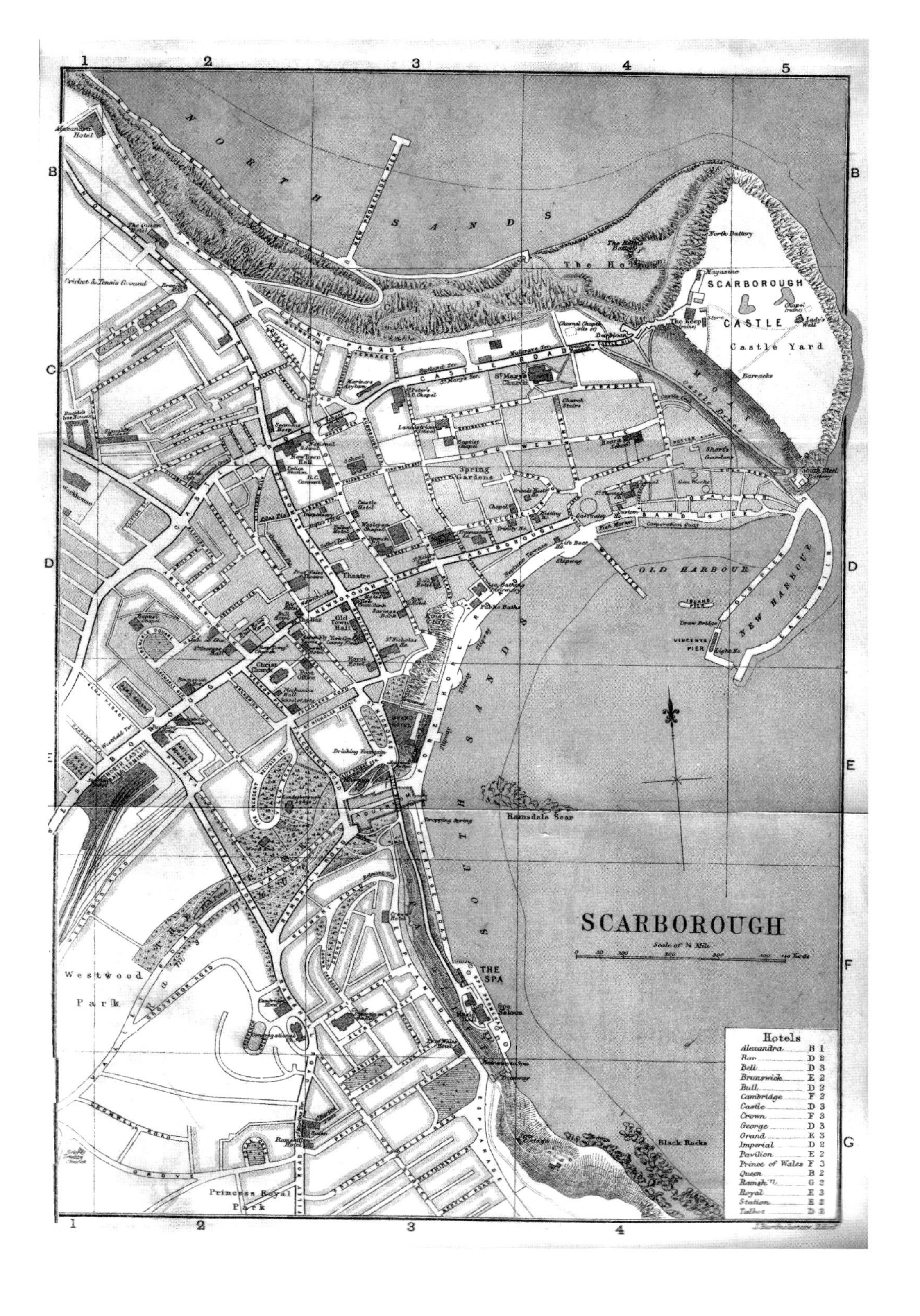
SCARBOROUGH
Scale of ¼ Mile
Hotels
Alexandra B 1
Bar D 2
Bell D 3
Brunswick E 2
Bull D 2
Cambridge F 2
Castle D 3
Crown F 3
George D 3
Grand E 3
Imperial D 2
Pavilion E 2
Prince of Wales F 3
Queen B 2
Royal E 3
Station E 2
Talbot D 3
NORTH SANDS
SOUTH SANDS
SCARBOROUGH CASTLE
Castle Yard
The Holms
North Battery
Magazine
Barracks
OLD HARBOUR
NEW HARBOUR
VINCENTS PIER
Ramsdale Scar
Black Rocks
THE SPA
Spa Saloon
Westwood Park
Princess Royal Park
Spring Gardens
Theatre
Old Town Hall
St. Mary's Church
Cricket & Tennis Ground
Workhouse

Then & Now
Scarborough

Colin Waters

TEMPUS

Frontispiece: A map of Scarborough in 1890, drawn before the Marine Drive was constructed and showing the 'New Promenade Pier' in the North Bay.

First published 2005

Tempus Publishing Limited
The Mill, Brimscombe Port,
Stroud, Gloucestershire, GL5 2QG
www.tempus-publishing.com

British Library Cataloguing in Publication Data.
A catalogue record for this book is available from the British Library.

ISBN 0 75243618 X

Typesetting and origination by Tempus Publishing Limited.
Printed in Great Britain.

Contents

Introduction

Scarborough's history is undeniably linked to its connection with the castle. It is known that a Roman military lookout was placed upon the promontory now occupied by the castle around AD 370. The Saxons built upon the Roman foundations and gave the area its modern name in the form of *Scearburg*, signifying a fort near the rocky scaur below, though some insist the name is derived from the nickname – *Skarthi* – of an eighth-century Viking named Thorgil who attacked the town. Whatever the truth, by the time these first Viking raids took place, signs of a permanent town settlement were already evident.

It was in 1066, the year of the Battle of Hastings, that forces of the Viking king Harold Hardrada attacked the town and left it and its fortifications in a state of ruin. Around 1136 the first substantial stone-built castle that stood on the site was founded by William le Gros, the third Earl of Albemarle, who was leader of the English army at the Battle of the Standard. When Henry II seized the town in 1154, le Gros was forced to flee and Henry ordered that the decayed castle be strengthened and rebuilt. The keep was constructed shortly after in 1158.

The first eyewitness account of Scarborough in ancient times was recorded in the mid-twelfth century by William of Newburgh. He describes the area below the castle as the place where 'the city begins'. It is possible that Scarborough at that time had quite a large population. It has been estimated that even in this early period there could have been as many as 3,000 people living within and outside the 'city wall' that is believed to have extended from the castle walls to Auboro' Street Gate and onwards to Bland's Cliff. From that point it descended down Merchant's Row to the bottom of Eastborough and circled round once more to join the castle walls beyond Quay Street. Moats, ditches, gateways and at least two drawbridges were to be found along the length of the wall. One drawbridge was sited at the castle entrance and another to the east of the present Market Hall at the top of St Sepulchre Street.

Around 1252 Henry III granted the burgesses of *Scardeburg* the right to collect duties from all merchants' ships and fishing vessels 'to make a new port with timber and stone'. It is interesting to note that another charter of that period described '*Scardeburgh*' as the *New Town* to distinguish it from the former main settlement at *Walesgrif* (Falsgrave).

The new stone castle was described as an 'unassailable citadel', though this did not stop attacks upon it over the years. The first occasion was in April 1312 when 300 men, mostly tenants from Pickering Forest, forced the surrender of Piers Gaveston, its governor. During this siege the Baronial army, led by Henry de Percy and the Earl of Warrene, cut off supplies for a period of three weeks while they camped on Bland's Cliff, watering their men from the spring that later became the Scarborough Spa. Six years later the castle escaped damage – though the town was destroyed – when Sir James Douglas attacked Scarborough with a raiding party that had come from Scotland by sea.

The next major period of conflict came in 1536 when the castle inhabitants were called upon by Sir Robert Aske to support the Pilgrimage of Grace, a rebellion that had been prompted originally by the dissolution of the monasteries but which had grown to reflect mass discontent against landlords and high prices of goods. The castle inhabitants on this occasion refused to give their support to the rebellion and, though the castle was besieged, they succeeded in seeing off their opponents.

When the proposal to marry Queen Mary I to the King of Spain was made public, Thomas Stafford sailed from France to Scotland and declared himself 'Protector of England'. He raised an army of men and marched into Yorkshire, eventually seizing Scarborough Castle in 1557. His tactics were unusual but successful. Thirty of his men, dressed as common farmers, hid under a pile of hay and, once through the gates, casually wandered around, disarming the castle guards one by one. The incident gave rise to a once common phrase: 'The Scarborough Warning – a word and a blow, but the blow comes first'.

Despite Stafford's easy victory, his success was short-lived. Within a week he and his men had surrendered to government officials. All were transported to the Tower of London where they were tried for high treason and beheaded.

Another siege of the castle commenced on 18 February 1644 when Sir John Meldrum attacked the defender Sir Hugh Cholmley. Meldrum died in the ensuing conflict and his place was immediately taken by Sir Matthew Boynton, who succeeded in bringing the castle inhabitants to such a state of hunger and scurvy through lack of food that they surrendered on 25 July 1645. The siege had lasted almost a year and a half. These were turbulent times and three years later it was the turn of Boynton to surrender the castle to Parliamentary forces. In August 1648, Colonel Bethel led yet another siege lasting four months and eventually succeeded in getting himself appointed governor of Scarborough Castle. By 1745 the castle buildings were being used as an ammunition store. Soldiers' barracks were erected the following year.

The last great assault on the castle came centuries later when, on 16 December 1914, two German warships bombarded the town for around twenty-five minutes, causing a great deal of damage and destroying the barracks and the coastguard station. Shells also damaged some of the walls and blew a large hole in the castle keep. The pier lighthouse, hotels, religious establishments, schools, private residences and businesses all suffered damage in one form or another.

Despite the troubled times that had affected the castle up to this point, the town had grown steadily from the mid-1700s onwards. An engraving of 1735 shows that the present town area at the base of the castle was largely devoid of buildings other than a small gathering of houses lying in the valley below St Mary's church. Grassed areas and gardens stood side by side with ships hauled upon the sands and a narrow quay skirted the bottom of the castle mound. No roadway ran along the shoreline at that time, though the original spa building was already in position.

The 1800s saw perhaps the town's largest period of growth. In 1811 the population of Scarborough was just under 7,500 while by 1891 it had increased to nearly 34,000. Scarborough became a Municipal Corporation in 1836 with Councillor Samuel S. Byron as its first mayor. The building of places of entertainment was encouraged to draw visitors, a typical 'diversion' being the twice-weekly summer balls. When a new theatre was built in Tanner Street (St Thomas Street) crowds flocked to see not only the performers but also its fashionable décor. Following the arrival of the railway in 1845 tourism became a leading means of income for local businesses. A museum was started in the 1860s and an aquarium in 1877.

The former maritime trades of fishing, shipbuilding, rope-making etc. were by now taking second place, though the herring fishing trade continued successfully well into the 1950s.

Today, the town's success relies mainly on commerce, much of it drawn from the continual stream of holidaymakers that return year after year. Scarborough has changed greatly from the days when staid Victorian ladies and gentlemen sought the benefits of spa waters and a quick dip in the ocean from a bathing machine. Today's visitors have altogether different expectations and, in true form, Scarborough continues to cater for their ever-changing needs.

Acknowledgements

Thanks are due to all the people who have assisted me in compiling this book by giving, loaning or suggesting old pictures or by giving permission to reproduce them. Acknowledgement must also be given to the original photographers who took these old photographs many years ago, many of whom I have been unable to trace and who must sadly remain anonymous. I extend my thanks to Mrs A. Thompson of the Windmill Hotel who kindly gave her permission to use the photograph and information from her hotel website; Brian and Kath Hepples for their assistance in gathering and verifying historical information for me; the security staff of the Brunswick Centre; and the two anonymous British Rail staff who agreed to have their photographs taken outside the railway station for this book. I must also thank the countless people of Scarborough who, without exception, readily assisted with help and information whenever I stopped them in the street with queries about buildings and locations. On a personal level I must thank my wife Sylvia, who, without complaint, trudged many miles around Scarborough, accompanying me and assisting me to take the modern photographs within these pages, often during inclement weather.

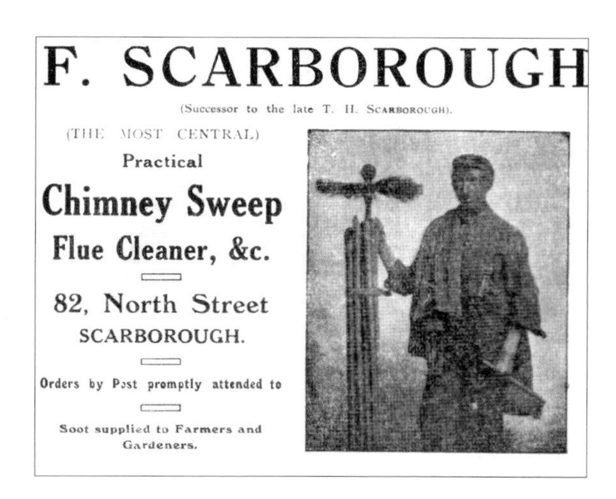

When a young F. Scarborough was pictured in this advertisement in 1933, chimney sweeping was still a dirty business. It would appear that his father, T.H. Scarborough, had recently died, though Mary Scarborough, presumably his mother, still lived at the address given in the advertisement, 82 North Street.

Chapter 1

Scarborough on the Move

Transportation in and around Scarborough has taken many forms over the years. Travelling the Filey Road by bus was a crowded affair when this group of flat-capped gentlemen were photographed outside of Scarborough railway station in the early 1900s. This particular vehicle had seven rows of wooden benches, each carrying four or five passengers, with a typical 'full load' of about thirty people. When in motion, both the men and the women would have to hold tight on to their hats and it was not unknown in those days for the driver to stop the bus a number of times during a journey in order for passengers to retrieve hats and caps that had blown off at various points along the route. It is interesting to see that at least one passenger, on the end of the third row from the front, had taken the precaution to cover his legs with a large blanket in order to protect himself from the draught.

This old picture shows another of the many buses that once congregated outside of the railway station doors. It may be one of Milburn's Motor Char-a-banc fleet that ran trips from Scarborough. The couple in the centre of the picture are both of eastern origin, showing that even in those early days foreign visitors were being drawn to the resort. It is interesting to note that the vehicle is fitted with a fixed starting handle and spoked solid rubber-tyred wheels. The station was the usual gathering place for both bus and rail passengers at that time. Today only taxicabs stop at the same spot. Around 1913, when the old picture was taken, various tourist rail tickets could be bought at Scarborough train station for those with limited budgets, while the more well-to-do visitors could buy a 'Thousand-Mile Ticket' for £5 5s. This was in fact a book of vouchers which could be used throughout the year by the purchaser or anyone he or she cared to give them to. Each ticket was charged at the rate of 1 ¼d per mile and could be used anywhere on the North Eastern Railway network.

Trams were also a popular means of travel in earlier days. When new tramway tracks were being laid beneath the footbridge on Valley Road, a local photographer captured the scene. Some of the workers involved in the work, together with supervisors and observers from the general public, gathered together for this picture. When comparing the scene with its modern equivalent, it can be seen that the road level at that time was quite flat, involving a relatively steep drop for the trams as they went over the brow of the hill under the bridge before dropping down towards the sea. Today a gentler slope is enjoyed by the motorist and cyclists who are pictured following the same route towards the marine drive and the harbour that can be seen in the background.

When this photograph was taken in 1929, United Automobile Co. ran a motorbus service from the railway station via Manor Road to Prospect Mount and the Briercliffe area in this small Chevrolet bus. The previous year, the company had bought a number of individual bus companies in the area, including Pioneer Buses, which ran between Scarborough and Whitby, Allan's Motor Services to Cloughton, and Rhine's Motors, which operated a town service. In that year they also expanded further by buying up Scarborough District Motors, Robinson's coaches and the People's Motor Services. Today's buses travel similar routes, but the old system of using a driver and a conductor, with his ticket machine around his shoulder, as seen in the old picture, has been replaced by the one-man-operated bus. It is interesting to note that in 1929, company rules stated that the wearing of uniforms was optional.

Below is an old photograph of one of the Scarborough District Motor coaches, a company that was taken over by United Automobile Services in 1929. It provided a service to York and back and is pictured outside the United bus garage near St Nicholas Parade where all vehicles were stored at night and where maintenance took place. At that time, United also carried parcels as well as passengers and some carried a letterbox for the convenience of the public. Strict timetables didn't exist and it was not unknown for people to hail the bus simply to post a letter or perhaps to buy cigarettes from one of the many cigarette machines carried on various routes. In this way buses provided a complete service to isolated communities, carrying passengers and mail, as well as providing for the needs of desperate smokers. The building in the picture, like the nearby former bus station once situated near the end of Valley Bridge, no longer caters for local bus transport but is currently used as a multi-storey car park.

The traffic that passes the railway station has changed greatly over the years. As can be seen when this old postcard was issued in the early 1900s, the main modes of transport were trams, horse-drawn vehicles and bicycles, though apart from the change in clothing and transport styles the scene remains remarkably similar today. The main differences to be noted are mainly in the area around the railway station frontage. At the time the earlier picture was taken that area would probably have been used for the dropping off and picking up of passengers using horse-drawn taxis. At a slightly later period it became a bus terminus, with the building to the immediate right of the old photograph serving as the railway station tearoom and café. In the distance, close to where the traffic lights now stand, can be seen an open-topped tram.

A group of unknown Scarborough railway station employees posed for this scratchy old picture during the early 1900s at a time when railway excursions and regular services kept drivers, guards, porters, signalmen and other employees busy from morn 'til night during the busy tourist season. It is interesting to note that only two of the men do not have moustaches and that a number of them carry watch chains, (the watch being as much part of their railway equipment as their flags, luggage trolleys and regulation cap and uniform). Despite the large number of trains entering and leaving Scarborough, services ran like clockwork. Timetables were strictly adhered to and advice and help for passengers were all very much part of the service. Today's staff are fewer and less formal in their dress and the wall notices once advertising excursions to far-off places have been replaced by formal details notifying users of the fact that vehicles will be wheel clamped and fined if they exceed the parking time limit.

THE
SCARBOROUGH
FLYER
60870

The Scarborough Flyer once offered one of the most prestigious and long-distance services to the town, sometimes running from London via York. It is pictured here in the early 1950s just before it entered Scarborough station. Similar services have been run ever since, though the old days of steam are virtually gone forever. Today's most famous train is the Trans-Pennine Express, pictured here just leaving the station. Apart from its distinctive colouring, it looks very much like all other trains and somehow does not attract the attention that the old 'Flyer' would have done in days gone by.

Train travel has always been a popular means of bringing tourists to the town since the railway arrived in the 1800s. In 1890 tickets to the town were available in first, second or third class carriages, with special cheap tourist tickets being available in all three classes. A typical tourist ticket at that time cost £3 1s from London in luxurious first class or £2 7s in second class. The third class fare was £1 14s. Passengers from Sheffield could obtain similar tickets for £1 3s 8d for first class travel, 19s 4d for second class, or 13s and 6d in the very basic third class carriages.

Transport of a different kind has always been popular with visitors to the foreshore. In 1890 one guidebook stated '... the Spa brings the South Foreshore Road to an abrupt end', though by the time the accompanying old postcard was taken the ever popular cliff tramway was carrying passengers up the face of the cliff side. By that time, it is clear that buildings had been erected to extend the foreshore esplanade. It is interesting to see also that the building at the foot of the tramway still has the same sign and that modern visitors, now as then, feel that the small fare to be paid for the ride far outweighs the disadvantage of climbing the 224 steps leading up to the top of the South Cliff.

In the early 1800s, when road travel was long and sometimes dangerous, Scarborough was a port of call for steam packets carrying goods and passengers from Edinburgh to London. At that time local businessmen Francis Hill and David Nicholson acted as agents for the *Tourist*, *City of Edinburgh* and the *James Watt*. In later years steam was used to propel fishing trawlers like the one moored to the left of this old photograph. The passenger steamboat seen leaving the harbour is the *White Lady*. It was possibly a sister ship of the *Royal Lady* that, around the 1920s, was operated by Thomas Rounde & Sons of Sandside. It took passengers to Robin Hood's Bay, Whitby, Filey and Bridlington. Though passenger boats still operate out of the port, as can be seen from the modern photograph, the steam trawlers are now just a memory.

With the coming of motor traffic, the new Marine Drive was officially opened in 1908, though, because of the lack of vehicles in the town, it was more of a 'Marine Walk' as can be seen from this old postcard. In it ladies in long gowns and big hats and carrying parasols to protect their complexions from the heat of the sun are accompanied by men wearing straw boaters or trilby hats, carrying walking canes. Ironically, when this modern photograph was taken the Marine Drive was again void of general traffic as it was closed to motor vehicles so that major building works could be undertaken. Some of the equipment being used can be seen in the modern photograph alongside, where a couple of lone walkers tread in the footsteps of the much larger crowds of former years.

Cars now travel where only walkers once strolled. On the summer's day captured in this old photograph taken about 1905, long white skirts, big hats and parasols were the order of the day for ladies, while men carried a walking cane and wore suits or blazers topped off with straw hats. Though slightly indistinct, this old photograph shows walkers on the beach dressed in less formal wear, indicating perhaps that the class system of the time was very much in evidence and that only those in 'proper attire' would promenade along the seafront. The location is the spa bandstand where chamber music or sometimes sea shanties would be played for the delight of visitors. Those seen sitting here are probably listening to one of these summer seaside concerts. Today the bandstand area has been extended and is now fitted with glass panels, while cars – not promenaders – travel around it.

Above is one of Boxwell's well-known grainy postcards showing the Central Tramway from the South Sands to St Nicholas Street. It was at this time that one of three such modes of transport were popular with visitors who did not want to climb the alternative routes by steep steps, footpaths or roadways. The fare at that time was 1d, a cost that was thought of as very reasonable. Today the tram still operates and, though the fare has risen to 45p, it is still considered a small sum to pay and proves a popular ride for adults and children alike.

Not far from the top of the tramway seen in the previous picture is the town centre where Newborough Bar once separated a lower area of the town from what is now the modern shopping area. In the centre of the old picture is a 'gallows sign' extending over the full width of the road, advertising the presence of the Bull Inn (to the left of the cart). The Bar itself does not have turrets, indicating that the print was made prior to 1843 when the archway was rebuilt. The windows within the Bar building are those of the town gaol. High up on the hill in the distance is the castle, with its long wall ending in a large building that served as soldiers' barracks. This building remained standing until 16 December 1914 when it was destroyed by shells fired from a German battleship. Modern rebuilding has obscured the view of the castle and vehicles are now excluded from what was once one of the main transport thoroughfares of old Scarborough.

This early postcard shows a later view looking down Scarborough's main shopping street towards the bottom of Newborough. It was originally produced in colour in a distinctively continental style. The card is believed to have been published by German printers and possibly was also available as a poster. It shows an elegantly dressed lady crossing the tramlines that ran down the middle of the street. None of the businesses in the picture are identifiable except for a branch of Boots the Chemist to the immediate right, where a tall Royal Mail letterbox stands at the corner of the street. Today's fashions are less elegant, though distinctly more serviceable considering the biting sea winds that sometimes blow through the town.

Chapter 2

Gone Forever

Though much of the town has changed or evolved over the years, there are many parts of the town that are gone forever. A modern blank wall in Cambridge Place now marks the place of an important part of Scarborough's past. In 1834 this was the site of Falsgrave 'Town' School, showing that even at that time the area was considered quite a separate entity from the main town of Scarborough. In 1821 it had a population of 345, which within ten years had grown to 391. A description of the area in 1834 stated that:

FALSGRAVE is a small village and township, in the parish of Scarborough, one mile from that town, [and] *is much resorted to by the visitors and inhabitants of Scarborough in the summer, having a subscription pleasure garden, established under the auspices of the Duchess of Leeds.*

A later entry of 1890 describes the National School:

All Saints' National School is situated between Falsgrave and Londesborough Roads, adjoining the church – the north wall of the school being the south wall of the church. The present school superseded a much smaller one, which was burnt down on the last Saturday in 1879. There is one large department, and an infants' room; also three class rooms. The whole giving accommodation for 400, with an average attendance of 390. In connection with the school is a library and penny bank.

This postcard shows the old Falsgrave School, *c.*1900. The building appears not to have altered much in the intervening years from the earlier sketch other than that the building shown to the right of the door on the previous print had been demolished and a low wall topped with iron railings had been put in place. It is not known who the man standing against the railing is, though it has been suggested that he was the head teacher at that time. To the left can be seen the local chapel and between them the entrance to the Strawberry Gardens. The buildings to be seen on the left of the modern picture were built on the site of the demolished chapel, while the tree in the foreground marks the position of the bowler-hatted man standing near the railings.

The large imposing building that holds Scarborough's Public Library is a far cry from the library facilities provided at Scalby School in earlier days. In the 1800s Scarborough had its own small library situated in the premises of Solomon William Theakstone, a man of vision who was born in York in 1810. He arrived in Scarborough aged eighteen and set up a range of businesses and public services including the library, newsroom, bookshops and stationery supplies. He founded the *Scarborough Gazette*, gave the town its first art gallery and began a publishing business, producing Scarborough's first real visitor's guide. This old engraving shows the building housing Theakstone's printers, public library and stamp office. It is believed to be the one described in 1860 as being in Bow Street, off Victoria Road, where we are told it was also used for billiards, services and meetings. A memorial window to Theakstone's wife Eleanor, who died in 1858 aged fifty-three, was placed in Scarborough's Christ Church in 1874.

When looking at the modern scene on Scarborough's seafront, it is hard to imagine that the spot was once the scene of a thriving shipyard with sailing ships being constructed and repaired on the sands at the foot of the castle mound. Though roughly drawn, the old picture captures the days of shipbuilding and associated trades such as rope-making and sail-making. In the 1800s these were already in decline. It is recorded that only six ships were built in 1825 and in 1840 only a single ship (perhaps the one shown in the sketch). Prior to its reliance on the tourist trade, Scarborough also had a flourishing import and export trade. The port once handled around 25,000 tons of goods per annum. Groceries came from London and coal from Newcastle, while ships from the Baltic brought timber and cloth. Wines and spirits arrived from other continental ports. The chief exports in earlier times were farm produce and salted fish.

In 1907 when this old picture was taken on the sands nearby, where the old shipbuilding yards once stood, beachside entertainment at Scarborough relied on musical concerts provided by Pierrots. They wore dress based upon similar entertainers in France. Generally this consisted of spotted clown-like costumes. The outfit was completed by the wearing of pointed white caps. An alternative formal style of outfit consisted of white flannel trousers and blazers, buckskin boots and a straw boater. Though these troupes of entertainers were to be found in all seaside towns on a seasonal basis, Scarborough was unusual in having them in 1907 as a strike was called by the newly formed union known as the VAF (Variety Artists' Federation) which affected many of the touring groups.

Today tourists expect more sophisticated entertainments such as the permanent funfair, Luna Park, which stands not far from the place where the Pierrots were photographed in earlier times, at the end of the seashore, close to the foot of Scarborough Castle.

Across the road from the big wheel in Scarborough's Luna Park fairground stood the bathing machine establishment of Weddel & Co., as featured on this illustration taken from an old letterhead. In the early 1800s there were just three official establishments. Each provided bathing machines for one shilling so as to protect the modesty of those undressing before entering the sea. For the shilling fee, each female would be provided with two attendants while males had the option of one or no attendants. Two of the three early establishments were run by a Dr William Harland and a surgeon named Travis, while the third was owned jointly by a Dr Thompson and a Mr McTurk. In addition the General Sea Bathing Infirmary, an organisation supported by public subscription, provided free bathing facilities for the sick and infirm. Today the steps and wooden footbridge seen in the old print have been replaced by a slipway and a modern road.

Within a short walk of Weddel's establishment, shown in the previous picture, a whole row of buildings have vanished from the scene. Sandside was greatly altered in the early 1900s when a number of buildings were demolished to open up the area at the side of the harbour. In the old picture taken in 1902 we can see many of the buildings beyond the Lancaster Inn that were removed during this period of redevelopment. As can be seen, a slight incline descended from the Lancaster Inn towards the harbour. This however was corrected during redevelopment and the road was levelled. Today's scene is quite different. There are no buildings to the right of the roadway and the way has been made clear as far as the funfair at the beginning of the Marine Drive beneath the castle mound. The Lancaster Inn still survives, though the architecture has been radically altered since the time when the earlier picture was taken.

Winding up behind the buildings shown in the two previous sets of pictures is the path to the castle. When this sketch was made, the remains of one of the castle drawbridges were still in existence and entry to the castle was free to all. The modern concept of admission charges wasn't introduced until modern times. George Fox (1624-1690), a shoemaker by trade and the founder of the Quaker movement, was imprisoned in the castle for a year at the time of Charles II. The castle must have been in a ruinous state even then, as he wrote that the room he was imprisoned in was '... much open, the wind drove in the rain so forcibly, that the water came over my bed, and ran about the room, so that I was glad to skim it up with a platter... most of my drink was water, with an infusion of wormwood'. It is also known that maintenance was carried out in 1745 when the barracks were repaired and were fitted out with twelve apartments to hold a regiment of 120 soldiers. Additional batteries were also added at that time to protect the town, two at the south and one on the north side of the castle yard. The remains of the tower holding the wooden drawbridge structure can still be seen centre-right in the modern picture.

The Tower on North Cliff

The development of the North Cliff as an extension of the fast-growing tourist resort began in 1844 when a row of boarding houses called North Marine Terrace was built alongside the Albion Corn Mill. In later years North Marine Terrace was given the more stately title of Queen's Parade and other buildings sprang up all around it. This rare old postcard shows the Spectacular Revolving Warwick Tower that was erected as a visitor attraction on the North Cliff in 1898. It stood over 150 foot (approximately 52 metres) in height and gave tourists a bird's eye view of the town, the castle and out to sea. Though the tower proved attractive to those visiting the town, locals, particularly those living nearby, were not altogether happy with the new addition to the scenery. After five years' exposure to the salt-laden winds blowing off the sea, the structure began to rust and the apparent lack of maintenance began to show. In 1907 it was deemed an eyesore and was consequently demolished. Today the garden fences of nearby buildings are all that remain of the site once visited by flocks of tourists.

The Promenade Pier in the North Bay is shown here at the time of its opening or at some time shortly afterwards. The iron pier, which was built by private enterprise at a cost of £16,000, eventually extended over 1,000 feet into the sea and was fitted with public benches along its entire length. Its construction began on 14 September 1866 and it was officially opened in 1868. The building at the end served as a lounge where chamber music was played. Entry to the pier cost 1d. By 1889, the pier had become rusty and unsightly and was sold for only £1,240. Walter Hudson, its new owner, refurbished the pier at a cost of over £10,000 and transformed the entrance by building shops, a café, ladies' cloakroom and 'retiring rooms' all lit by the 'newfangled' electric lighting. In January 1905 a destructive storm caused the pier to be dismantled. Today, a similarly styled modern café stands not far from the same spot.

Scarborough once boasted two outdoor pools, the popular North Bay pool and this one in the South Bay which was built in 1915 at a cost of £5,000. Today the site, having become derelict, has been grassed over. The pool was seen as a modern-day replacement for the 'health-giving' dips in the sea which first became popular with the aristocracy, but later with everyone, after doctors advised that sea bathing was a health-giving pastime. Males were advised to bathe for five minutes before breakfast while women, children and invalids should bathe more often but only for two minutes each time. It was common, even in the 1800s for men to bathe without clothing, while women wore specially adapted frocks. The invention of 'bathing costumes' developed from crude alterations to ordinary clothing whose design progressed to specially designed gowns and swimwear that quickly caught on as manufacturers produced outfits especially for the purpose of swimming in the sea.

Another of Scarborough's well-loved amenities was the aquarium. Its glass canopy entrance stood below the footbridge over Valley Road. As can be seen in this typically grainy Boxell & Co. postcard, the ticket house stood to the extreme right of the road, looking towards the sea. To enter the aquarium it was necessary to descend below the level of the road where underground rooms held the exhibits. This underground area has been used to house a number of attractions over the years, including a miniature world inhabited by real-life dwarfs who in the daytime spent their time living in tiny mock houses and shops for the amusement of the public, a use that would be seen as politically incorrect in this modern age. Gardens and flowerbeds now hide any signs that the aquarium ever existed.

The building of the Grand Hotel at the end of the footbridge shown in the previous picture entailed the demolition of the row of cottages to be seen to the left of the old picture. In one of these cottages Anne Brontë, of the famous literary family, died. Anne and two of her sisters were born at Thornton (now part of Bradford). Her father, Patrick (1777-1861) was an Irish-born handloom weaver who took Holy Orders and became vicar of Haworth in Yorkshire, while her mother, Maria, *née* Branwell, was a Cornish woman. Of the couple's six children, only four, Anne, Charlotte, Patrick Branwell and Emily Jane survived childhood. All became writers of prose and poetry. The best known of these are Charlotte's novel *Jane Eyre* and Emily's novel *Wuthering Heights.* Anne produced two lesser-known novels, *Agnes Grey* and *The Tenant of Wildfell Hall.* In 1848, both Patrick Branwell and Emily died of consumption and Anne became so ill with the same condition that Charlotte, who was also ill, decided to bring her to Scarborough in the hope that the sea air would provide a cure. Unfortunately within weeks, on 28 May 1849, Anne died and was buried in St Mary's graveyard in Scarborough, where her gravestone can still be seen. Charlotte survived another six years.

This old postcard shows St Mary's church with the now vanished old drinking fountain that was once well used by passers-by and local householders. Close to the site of the old fountain, on the opposite side of the road and closer to the castle, once stood a charnel chapel, probably attached to the original Cistercian establishment here. The fountain was erected in 1860 as a memorial to local historian and museum founder Thomas Hinderwell, whose grave lies close to the wall within the churchyard. The fountain was fed from a natural spring known as the Lady's Well, in nearby Castle Garth. Prior to 1850, the south transept of the aisle of the church was known as Farrar's Aisle and was used as a local grammar school. The *parvise* or priest's chamber above the south porch was set up as a museum around 1912. The fountain is not the only thing missing from the scene today. As can be seen from the modern picture, many of the old gravestones have disappeared also.

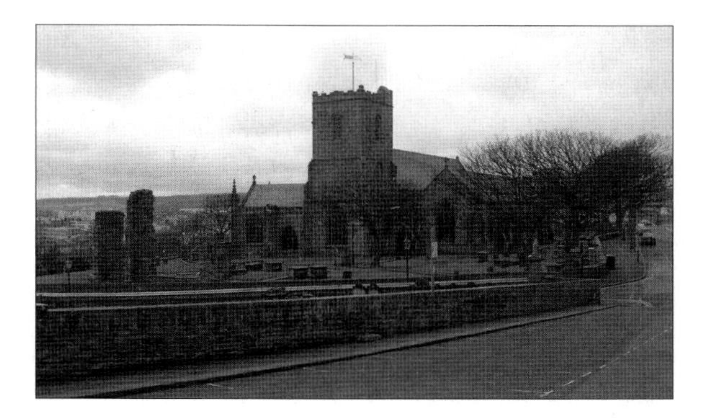

From the church, it is a short walk to the top of Auborough Street where there is nothing now to indicate that it once served as one of the main gates through the town walls. This rare view of two buildings from Scarborough's ancient past was drawn around 1817, at or near the same spot. It shows on the left the Amicable Society School with the town pinfold (where stray animals were kept until the owner collected them) in the centre. The building on the right was the home of the town pinder and his family. It would be his job to round up any stray animals and to look after them until such time as a fee was paid for their retrieval. To the left of the picture are four posts marking the point known as Auborough Gate where a drawbridge once provided access over a ditch. The archway that guarded this point of entry to the castle may have been attached to the group of buildings in the old picture.

In medieval times Newborough Bar or Gate formed another defensive point in the town walls. A drawbridge crossed a wide ditch at this point through a single arched gateway. The buildings forming the gate served as the town prison. The Bar was rebuilt in 1843 in this more architecturally aware style with turrets on each side, as this picture shows. The building on the right, showing a sign with a horse's head upon it, was, at the time of painting, the Nag's Head public house. It later changed its name to Miller's (perhaps after the landlord). It undertook a further name change in later years, being called the Old Bar before receiving its last name of the Huntsman. All buildings on the side of the arch leading to the sea were termed 'Within the Bar', while those through the archway leading up to the top of the present town were 'Without the Bar'. When North Street was built, a number of buildings to the right of the picture were demolished.

This view of Newborough Bar from the other side (Westborough) shows the Bull Hotel and Vaults situated to the extreme left of the old picture shown above. The public house, which was almost directly opposite Huntriss Row, had a coach yard at its rear. It was rebuilt in 1891 and took the name of the Balmoral. In the same vicinity were the premises of J. Blakeborough, ironmongers (the last building on the left before the arch). Opposite stood Kirkness's jewellers and the Scarborough House & Estate Agency and the Assembly Rooms on Huntriss Row. In those days pedestrians would have been used to the constant clip-clop sound of horses' hooves and probably never envisaged that the day would come when the street would become a modern pedestrian precinct, devoid of all traffic.

Since time immemorial, there has always been a market at or near the same site as the present Market Hall. Today's large building, with its associated vaults, is a far cry from the vanished stalls, butchers, shops and booths that would have been in existence in earlier times. This undated painting shows the old market, probably in the 1700s, with a number of open-air stalls with their awnings and a conical building which was probably the market booth where the market inspector would collect his fees. The medieval-style building centre left has a sign saying 'Cass – Butcher', while to the extreme right of the picture on the stone building another sign can be seen advertising Rowntree's shop.

In 1858 a competition was held to design a new workhouse under the Poor Law Union Act to house Scarborough's less well-off residents. The chosen design incorporated accommodation for up to 400 inmates, as well as offices and ancillary buildings. There was also an infirmary for the sick. The winning design was submitted by two York architects, George and Henry Styan, and the building was completed at a cost of £12,000 and was sited between Dean Street, now called Dean Road, and Victoria Street. It opened on 4 December 1859 with around ninety inmates, including men and women of all ages, families with children and the very aged. With the 1948 Health Act the building became St Mary's Hospital. The building is still used today by the NHS as the Ellis Centre, though only the row of buildings fronting the road, seen in the modern picture, now remains, the rest having been demolished.

The dramatic sight of Holbeck Hall Hotel sliding slowly into the sea was flashed around the world by television in 1993 as the unstable cliffs slowly gave way, taking with them the hotel and much of the garden area below. Today the site is just a green slope where the mudslide has become grassed over, giving a view of the buildings behind. The first indication of the landslip took place on the evening of 3 June 1993. Though this was witnessed by walkers on the beach, apparently no one thought it significant enough to report it at the time. At midnight, the hotel manager noticed that the rose garden had sunk by 4 feet in depth and, from that point onward, the hotel slowly began to slide towards the sea. The two pictures alongside are taken from approximately the same viewpoint, showing just how much of the original cliff disappeared.

Before the landslip mentioned on the previous page, Holbeck Hall and its nearby gardens were an attraction to visitors from far and wide. The hotel can be seen here on the extreme right of the old picture, standing high above the cliffs, with panoramic views out to sea. In the first days of June 1993 the building and its reputation as a desirable place to stay came to an abrupt end when the cliffs below it started to subside. Luckily, because the landslip took place over a number of days, staff members and guests were able to be evacuated and no injuries were sustained. Today the scene in the once extensive Holbeck Gardens is very different, as can be seen from the modern picture looking towards another house nearby, with little of the once decorative gardens and paths remaining.

Chapter 3

The South Bay

The fishing fleet are seen here arriving back at port in the morning after a night's fishing. Some of these appear to be 'Penzance men', a type of fishing boat that was common in these waters up until the First World War when fleets of ships would travel up the east coast from Cornwall following the shoals of fish. The pier lighthouse can be seen in the distance on St Vincent's Pier. This lighthouse once served as home to the lighthouse keeper. Its last residents were Captain and Mrs R.E. Andrews. A memorial seat to them stands on the pier next to the building.

This old illustration of the South Bay is one of the oldest in existence. Drawn in 1735, it gives us a true idea of what Scarborough looked like in earlier times and shows the church of St Mary as it once would have looked. At the far left of the picture is the first spa building, known then as Dicky's Castle after its first governor Richard Dickinson (inset) who was a sufferer of acromegaly, the same affliction suffered by Joseph Merrick the 'elephant man'. Arthur Rowntree of Scarborough described Dickinson as 'one of the most deformed pieces of mortality I ever saw and of the most uncouth manner of speech'. Close to the spa a path winds up St Nicholas cliff, past the ruins of St Nicholas' church, then just a mound of stones. In the distance there is little in the way of quays or piers. A number of sailing ships are pulled up out of the water for repair on the extensive sands below the castle mound.

Though in early times Scarborough largely advertised itself as a place of recreation for sophisticated adults, children were not altogether forgotten. At the extreme end of the bay close to Holbeck Gardens, a facility was built especially for children, known as 'Children's Corner'. Here children could be brought, and sometimes left, to enjoy themselves under the eye of trained staff who provided a range of cheap but enjoyable diversions in a safe, clean environment matching the town's unblemished reputation for 'cleanliness and style'. In the early 1900s, we are told that in Scarborough '... there is nothing, except now and again an inevitable fishy odour caused by the herring trade, to offend the most sensitive nostril, while the more modern parts of the town are kept scrupulously clean.' Many of the chalets seen in the old postcard have now vanished to be replaced by other buildings, and the once popular Children's Corner is now a shadow of its former self.

The nearby popular Clock Tower Café, close to the spa, is pictured here as it was in the 1950s and as it is today. The 1950s saw a number of other changes to the spa and immediate area around it. In 1954 a glass screen was erected around the bandstand for an ice show and was left in place. The following year the ballroom was enlarged and altered. A new floor was constructed costing £2,000 and in 1957 the spa was purchased from the Cliff Bridge Co. by the Council at a cost of £110,000. 1958 saw the opening of the new Spa Restaurant and later, in the 1960s, work was begun on further alterations and improvements in order to carry out a complete restoration at a staggering cost of £3 million. Additional expensive improvements have been made since that time.

A Dr Robert Wittie is said to have unintentionally launched Scarborough as Britain's first real seaside resort after he published a booklet called *Scarborough Spaw* in 1660 and advocated its medicinal 'cistern' waters as a cure for virtually everything. He could never have imagined that an impressive spa building would have been erected on the site of the original 'cistern'. This old view of the spa looking up towards the top of the cliff probably dates from the early 1930s. Despite being taken out of season and just after the tide had receded it reflects the constant popularity of the beach at that time with children and adults alike. The modern picture taken at the same time of the year, shows that this part of the beach is now less popular with winter visitors. It also gives a clear indication of how the bandstand has been transformed with a glass enclosure.

If Dr Wittie was credited with first publicising the curative properties of Scarborough's medicinal springs, the actual discovery of the springs is attributed to a Mrs Elizabeth (or Tomazyn?) Farrar or Farrow (accounts vary). Around 1620 she is said to have recognised the medicinal value of the waters by their brown colour. The newly celebrated mineral water 'springs' later became known as 'wells' before being given an air of respectability by changing their name to 'spaws'. There were in fact two of these, a southern saline spa and a northern chalybeate one. As their fame spread, 'well-to-do' visitors began to pay 7s 6d for a season ticket to use them. In 1737 the spa was attracting around a thousand visitors per annum until a storm destroyed the springs temporarily before a cliff fall demolished them completely. Luckily a group of enterprising locals successfully set out to rediscover the springs and once more brought them into public use. These two views, then and now, show the same scene from the same angle with the bandstand to be seen to the right.

When this miniature postcard (dating from the period between the two world wars) was produced, Pierrots were still performing to the gathered crowds in Scarborough. Fashions had moved on somewhat and both clothing and the type of entertainment sought by visitors were becoming a little more sophisticated. Bathing machines had already disappeared from the beach and two-piece swimming costumes were beginning to appear. These were generally worn by wealthy women who had become used to this type of attire during their visits to Mediterranean resorts. Their appearance met with disapproval in some quarters but in general became accepted as a sign that the resort was attracting the sophisticated visitors that it had always aspired to.

The spa buildings were designed by Thomas Verity as a replacement for the former structure destroyed in a fire in 1876. They were opened on 2 August 1880 by the Lord Mayor of London at a cost of over £70,000. The spa water (one penny a glass, hot or cold) did not impress everyone. The following conversation between Samuel Weller and John Smauker is recorded in a local guidebook of the time:

Have you drunk the waters Mr Weller? – Yes replied Sam.
What did you think of 'em sir?
I thought they was particularly unpleasant.
Ah! You disliked the Killybeate [chalybeate] *taste, perhaps?*
I don't know about that – I thought they'd a very strong flavour o' warm flat irons!

When these formally dressed visitors promenaded past the spa building in 1913 they were unaware that the devastating First World War was only a year away. Today the promenade, seen in the modern picture from the south, has been completely altered. Cars now travel where the well-dressed crowds of past times once congregated.

Sea bathing was considered a cure for many diseases and a preventative of others. However a warning was given in the 1800s that, 'When the bathing does not produce a moderate glow after quitting the water; when the chilling sensation continues; when the extremities become cold, the spirits languid, the head disordered, or the appetite impaired, it may be concluded that bathing is rather doing harm than good'. Children in the 1950s had no such concerns, as pleasures were simple and cheap. Buckets and spades could be bought for pennies from any of the seaside shops lining the foreshore and paddling brought hours of pleasure to children and adults alike. The two children in the old picture with the pier and lighthouse in the background are unidentified but appear to be obtaining much pleasure with their shared bucket and spade. No doubt their parents would later treat them to a donkey ride or to an ice cream sandwich or cornet, before making their way home.

The Spa Terrace, steps and gardens can be seen in the two accompanying photographs, though the entertainment provided in the adjacent spa buildings has altered somewhat over the years. Many visitors still use the spa and frequent the surrounding area with its hillside walks and gardens, particularly the nearby Italian gardens created by the Scarborough Borough surveyor and engineer Harry Smith who held that post between 1897 and 1933. Others now choose to sample the delights to be found further along the bay where funfair rides, amusement arcades, public houses and other delights of a modern seaside resort attract the majority of today's crowds.

The spa buildings have altered vastly since the publication of Dr Wittie's book in 1660. This is mainly due to early visionaries who saw that the spa buildings could be enlarged for other purposes. Before long a new industry was born catering not only for the health needs of visitors, but also for their entertainment and accommodation. As the spa developed as a place of entertainment, its buildings began a constant cycle of rebuilding and change. A more distant view of the central bandstand from the beach shows just one of these developments. It has now been enclosed as part of today's main spa buildings structure. The tower to the left has also vanished, having been swallowed up by the new structure to be seen in the modern buildings.

This early 1900s illustration shows the spa and the 'South Cliff Tramway' together with its large advertising poster proclaiming, '224 STEPS AVOIDED FOR 1d'. No doubt a single penny was considered a cheap price to pay in order for visitors to reach the top of the cliff without getting out of breath. The local guidebook from which this picture is taken shows that the old bathing machines to be seen in the distance were considered expensive, ancient and cumbersome: 'The bathing is good on both shores and the machines as cumbrous and ugly as elsewhere and at a price! Nine Pence… It is possible that they are the same "chariots" as were described more than a century ago in *Humphrey Clinker.* Anyone the inventor of a bathing machine endurable either to look at or ride in, would make a fortune.' The picture was entitled 'The Sands', though, as is shown in this modern picture, taken in December 2004, much of the sand familiar to summer visitors disappears during the winter period.

The rough winter seas that remove the sand from the beaches is also responsible for emergency situations at sea off Scarborough's coastline. The old picture alongside shows one of Scarborough's old rowing lifeboats with its brave crew preparing to rescue a stricken ship. It is not known whether the scene – which is taken from an old poster – represents an actual rescue or if the poster was produced as a general sales item, perhaps to raise funds for the maintenance of the lifeboat. In 1933 the Royal National Lifeboat Institute, Scarborough branch, listed F.P. Morgan of St Nicholas Street as its honorary secretary and J. Owston as lifeboat coxon. Today's modern lifeboat is launched down a specially constructed shipway and is kept in the building pictured here on Scarborough's foreshore.

Many of those that face the perils of the sea each day are local fishermen. When the accompanying hazy old photograph was taken in the 1920s, Scarborough's fishing industry was based mainly on catching herring. These were sold in 'cran' weights and were carried in handmade wicker baskets. The two fishermen dressed in traditional flat caps and oilskin aprons have not been identified. Later in the 1950s scores of Scottish herring girls visited the town to gut or 'gip' the herrings before packing them into barrels so that they could be despatched throughout the land. Today, fishing is no longer the multi-million pound industry it once was. Though fishing boats are now fitted with echo sounders and satellite navigation, fishing quotas have severely limited catches so that families who for centuries had provided workers for the industry have turned their hands to other trades. Some still fish from small boats such as that shown in the modern picture.

This rare old postcard, dated 1909, was produced in colour and shows Scottish fisher-lasses at their work on the fish pier while sailors from the fishing boats attend to the ropes in the background. Above them stand locals and visitors dressed in long flowing dresses and large hats. The pier must have been a very smelly place at that time as the offal produced in the gutting of the fish was simply thrown into the harbour, much of it scattering on the ground in the process. Today more hygienic processes are in place, as can be seen in this modern picture where a worker is seen hosing down the area following the daily activities.

Today's fish quay is a much less hectic place in these modern times. The old picture shown here dates from the 1920s and shows a man in the centre of the picture emptying fish from a wicker basket into one of the many wooden fish boxes lined up for the purpose along the quayside. To his left is a man standing over a wooden fish barrel while in the background can be seen a heavy-duty weighing scale. Though the costumes have changed over the centuries, such scenes would have been familiar in the town as early as the Middle Ages when a fish market was held regularly on the beach. Such was the town's constant connection with the sea that in later years disabled fishermen and seamen were provided with a retirement home on the road to North Sands. This was managed by Trinity House and was funded by a tax of 6d levied on each vessel entering the port of Scarborough.

In 1929, Scarborough's fleet had a number of steam vessels used in the fishing trade. Some of the distinctive tall chimneys can be seen here on the boats just after they had arrived back in port. The one to the left carries the registration SH136, indicating that it was a Scarborough vessel. Other registration letters that would have been common in the harbour at that time include WY (Whitby), HL (Hartlepool), SN (South Shields), SSS (North Shields) and from further afield YH (Yarmouth) and PZ (Penzance). As can be seen, today's fleet is much smaller, not just in the quantity of boats fishing from the harbour, but also in the physical size of many of the boats moored at the fish quay.

Some of the earliest postcards depicting Scarborough were produced by Boxall & Co. Though roughly printed and of relatively poor quality, they did manage to capture images of the town that might otherwise have not survived. This old picture illustrated above is from one such postcard and shows the West Pier with its row of open stalls selling fish, crabs and other seafood. Behind them are stacked wooden barrels used for packing fish in ice. Though the picture is not dated, the absence of motor transport and the horse-drawn vehicles in the distance give the scene some antiquity. Today the scene is distinctly recognisable, though with some subtle changes such as the provision of modern covered-in fish stalls and the light-controlled pedestrian footway to cross what is now a very busy thoroughfare.

This old postcard shows a passenger steamer, moored near the St Vincent's pier lighthouse. It is believed to be the *Emu*, a vessel that ran a regular service in the early 1900s between Scarborough and Whitby. Today's lighthouse looks out over moored private yachts, indicating a new leisure industry that has developed since those earlier days. The earliest of the town's piers that can be verified was the East Pier of 1252. It is likely that the pier was in reality only a rough breakwater. The modern pier extensions date back to 1732, during the time of George II, when it was felt necessary to enlarge the town's sea defences. A duty of halfpenny per chauldron of coals was once imposed on all Newcastle coal-carriers. Additional duties were imposed on other imported or exported goods. With the money obtained from these fees, the piers were extended to 1,200 feet in length. In addition a new pier was later built using immense local stones from White Nab quarry.

ANTIQUES
SALE
SALE

Looking out over the bay for centuries has stood 'King Richard's House', reputedly the former residence of King Richard III when he stayed in the town in 1484/5 accompanied by Queen Anne and at a time when he granted the town a new constitution declaring 'the town of Scardeburgh and the manor of Wallesgrave' (Falsgrave) an independent county under the governorship of a mayor, sheriff and twelve aldermen. However, the status was not recognised by future monarchs and some time following the death of King Richard the town reverted to its original status as part of the county of York. It has been speculated that this old house once formed part of a larger mansion or even of an estate. In the late 1800s it served as a blacksmith's shop and has since had many uses, including that of a museum. The building is now a restaurant. This old picture was probably taken around 1946 and shows the building next door, No. 34, in use as an antiques shop.

When this old postcard was issued showing the start of Marine Drive at the end of the South Bay, motor vehicles were few and far between. Despite this, the local authorities had sufficient foresight to build Marine Drive to cope with the expected traffic of the future. The picture was probably taken sometime between the two world wars. Though the scene has altered little, today more motor cars than pedestrians use the route. It is interesting to note the distinctive building with its pointed tower still stands at the start of Marine Drive, though as can be seen its location is now slightly different. In recent years a traffic roundabout was placed nearby and work continues to take place in order to modernise and upkeep the Marine Drive area.

Chapter 4

All in a Day's Work

One of Scarborough's early traders was John Jackson who owned a tailors, outfitter and boot-selling business on Queen Street in 1910. Unlike most traders, John appears to have decided to have his portrait advertised instead of a picture of his shop as in this example where he is shown posing for the camera in a military uniform complete with fancy trimmings with a neatly waxed moustache. John Jackson's premises were at 20 Queen Street with another shop at 54 Falsgrave Road. Whether it was fact or vanity is not recorded, but this particular advertisement announces, 'You all know the noted tailor, outfitter & boot factor of 20 Queen Street and 54 Falsgrave Rd. Scarborough. Why Yes! It's John Jackson'. It is not known how long Jackson owned these premises, but by 1933 Frederick N. Slingsby occupied the Queen Street premises, while a Mr A. Scott was at the shop at 54 Falsgrave Road.

THE SCARBOROUGH PICTORIAL

WEDNESDAY, MARCH 3, 1915. ONE PENNY.

SCARBOROUGH'S GREAT FIRE -- SOUVENIR NUMBER.

THE REMNANT!

This pair of pictures shows the same plot at the corner of Market Street and Queen Street. In the modern picture, the distinctive architecture of the new Boyes Store with its well-known clock tower stands proudly on the site of the former Remnant Warehouse destroyed in 1915. As can be seen, the fire was featured prominently on the front page of local newspaper of that time, the *Scarborough Pictorial*. It is dated Wednesday 3 March 1915 and is advertised as *Scarborough's Great Fire Souvenir Number*, showing just how big an event the disaster was considered at the time. The destroyed warehouse had been run by the local Boyes family, who continue to own the business today. Earlier in 1890, William Boyes Junior, son of William Senior, was described in a local trade directory as a 'general and fancy draper, remnant & job stuff dealer' with a 'Remnant Warehouse at Market Street'. At that time William Boyes Junior lived at Chester Villa in Oak Road.

A fuzzy sepia photograph from 1915 shows all that remains of what became of the building with people standing before the twisted shell of the Remnant Warehouse. Also destroyed in the fire was the Queen Street chapel and many nearby buildings were also threatened. Here men who formed the fire crew can be seen posing outside the smoking ruins. Behind them broken walls and girders twisted by the heat of the fire are all that remain of the building, which had been the town's biggest and most popular store. Not to be outdone, the building was quickly rebuilt and in its place stands the 'new' Boyes department store which carries on the tradition of its predecessor to this day.

Those working in the lighthouse had to flee for their lives in December 1914 when fires broke out in a number of Scarborough buildings as, unexpectedly, the town came under fire from a German battleship moored off the town. During the bombardment, the lighthouse took a direct hit, with a shell blowing a great hole in it and causing the staff working inside to flee for their lives. The building was so badly damaged that it had to be rebuilt, though this didn't take place for many years. It was officially reopened in 1931 by the town mayoress, Mrs J.W. Butler. The Royal Hotel, Grand Hotel, Prince of Wales Hotel, the Town Hall and other local buildings were also hit, though the shells fell further afield also. It is said that the most distant bomb damage was to a farmhouse that stood three miles inland. The railway station remained unscathed though houses nearby were damaged and a shop was set on fire in Eastborough. Prospect Road, Hanover Road and Barwick Street also suffered damage and a café on the promenade took a direct hit with a shell. The surprise attacks on Scarborough, Whitby and Hartlepool caused outrage throughout the country and an army recruitment office, set up in St Nicholas Street, did a roaring trade after posters appeared in all three towns proclaiming 'Men of Yorkshire, join the new army and help avenge the murder of innocent women and children in Scarborough, Hartlepool and Whitby. Show the enemy that Yorkshire will exact a full penalty for this cowardly slaughter. ENLIST TODAY'.

Another casualty of the bombardment by German shells was the antique shop and silversmiths premises of Charles S. Smith, opposite Clair & Hunt's. Though Smith and his staff were counting their blessings that they had escaped death and injury, others were not so lucky. It later emerged that a hairdresser's wife was encouraging two neighbours to take shelter in her cellar when a shell hit a nearby stone pillar before glancing off it and killing her instantly. The wife of another tradesman in St Columbus Ravine died of her injuries when a shell hit her while she was rushing downstairs to her husband in the shop. Her husband was almost buried by the debris. On South Street today, all evidence of the premises of Charles Smith are gone forever, all that remains is a fenced-off thin strip and a narrower pavement.

Two men were killed on South Street during the German bombardment of the town. One was Leonard Ellis, a porter working at Clair & Hunt's premises (opposite the premises shown in the previous picture). Harry Frith also died at the same time. He was a driver for Land & Co. and was in the vicinity at the time. Luckily the rest of the streets on the South Cliff were relatively empty when the attack took place. Many people were still in bed and later emerged unconcerned, commenting to their neighbours about the terrible thunderstorm that had woken them. Today there is no sign that the building once used by Clair & Hunt was ever damaged and the shop now serves as the premises of a car parts company. The building directly to its left in both pictures was, at the time of the bombardment, a bank.

In 1901 J.L. Hopwood ran his family wholesale and retail grocery business from the premises known as Victoria House, 3 and 4 Queen Street, just a little way down the street and at the opposite side of the road from Boyes, whose great fire devastated much of the corner block opposite fourteen years later in 1915. Hopwood's business was one of many traditional old-fashioned provision merchants to be found in the town at that time. They would sell loose tea, freshly ground coffee beans, dairy products, ham, bacon and other meats. They also conducted a second business at 84 Castle Road where confectionary was sold on a wholesale and retail basis. This pictorial illustration, taken from an old almanac, when compared with the modern view, shows that apart from the ground floor, the premises have altered little over the intervening years.

The distinctive pillars over the top right and left windows still carry plaques telling us that the building was erected in 1899. Today's building is used for the sale of motoring requisites and accessories. It is interesting to note how the use of telephones has increased over the years. Today's business uses an eleven-figure number, whereby Hopwood's had the distinctive telephone number, Scarborough 0200.

The Windmill Hotel in Mill Street, Scarborough stands as a splendid example of how redundant heritage buildings can be put to modern use without spoiling their appearance. The site has been used for working windmills for at least 400 years and the present mill dates back to 1704 when it was rebuilt. It ceased to be driven by wind power in 1898 when the mill was modernised and it began to be powered by a gas turbine. It continued to grind corn until 1927 when it ceased production. Over the following years it was used for storing agricultural seeds and it even served as a newspaper distribution centre. Luckily plans to demolish it in 1998 were foiled and eventually the building was turned into a hotel and was listed as a Grade II industrial building. The hotel's present owners, Angela and Roland Thompson, have lovingly restored the mill and have even incorporated a toy museum within the building. The old picture alongside dates from the late 1800s and shows the building in its heyday when corn was being ground on a regular basis. To the right can be seen part of the mill workers' cottages. Today's scene is remarkably similar, though the cottages have now been demolished.

Perhaps the mill on the opposite page ground corn harvested by the farmer in this old picture? The back of the photograph taken on an unknown farm near Scarborough says simply 'Summer Hols! – Scarborough'. It is a sad fact that we are all guilty of not recording details on the back of photographs. Such was the case with this old picture, leaving us with the question of whether the children were on their school holidays, helping dad with the harvest, or whether they were children from elsewhere, spending their holiday on a farm. The style of dress and the horse-drawn thresher appear to date the photograph to a period in the very early 1900s. In the background, a simple thatched farmhouse with a single chimney gives what may be the only tantalising clue to the farm's location.

Today's mechanised farming may be faster and more profitable, though no doubt many older members of the farming community would give their right arm to return to the simpler life our ancestors knew in the past.

Much of today's population work in the high street shops or in bigger establishments such as the Brunswick Centre built in 1991. The building arose from a block of demolished businesses that previously existed on the same site, including Rowntree's store, seen here decorated to celebrate the Coronation of Edward VII in 1902. Today's high street stores now sell products from around the world, an opportunity that occurred rarely in the past, though foreign trinkets were available at Scarborough's regular fairs. It is not known which of the Scarborough Fairs the popular folk song refers to, but it is probably a reference to one of two early events that were held annually. One of these was on Holy Thursday (the day before Good Friday) and another on Martinmas (11 November). These would be mainly cattle and produce fairs but would also feature market stalls, fairground rides and sideshows for the entertainment of the local population.

Chapter 5

Leisurely Pursuits

Much of Scarborough's charm lies in its wide variety of pursuits suited to those who prefer leisure and pleasure rather than the more hectic attractions of a seaside resort. This applies to locals and visitors as this charming picture shows. Fishing for frog spawn was once a common pursuit in earlier times when school classes would provide a water tank so that the children could watch the tadpoles develop into full grown frogs. History does not record the names of these three young boys, though a note on the back tells us that the location is the Mere at Scarborough. The scene sadly reflects a lost era when childhood pursuits were simpler than those of the present day and when all boys dressed very much like their fathers. All three are wearing shorts, as long trousers were not worn at that time until a boy attended senior school. The picture was probably taken in the 1940s, although because fashions changed little in those times, the photograph could equally have been snapped ten years later. The flat hat of the boy on the left and the under-smock just showing beneath the jumper of the lad in the middle, may indicate that they were both sons of fishermen. It is also interesting to note that the two boys on the right are wearing heavy boots.

The tranquillity of Valley Gardens with its boating lake and fountain is captured here in an old view looking towards the sea. It dates from before the bridge was widened in 1928. The Valley Bridge was originally one of the bridges over the River Ouse at York but was brought to Scarborough in 1865. The Valley Gardens were described in 1928 as '… one of the beauty spots of Scarborough' and were, before modern traffic, a quiet place of solitude where families would gather to feed the swans and to picnic on benches provided nearby. The lake in the picture was known in 1914 as 'The Duck Pond' though it was considered big enough for rowing boats to be available for hire at that time. Today's scene is quite similar, though the rowing boats, swans and fountain are no more.

It was the borough surveyor and engineer of Scarborough from 1897 to 1933, Harry Smith, who was responsible for the construction of the Italian Gardens, situated close to the spa and the Esplanade. He would be pleased to see that his creation still looks very similar today. Here men wearing the once popular straw hats and carrying walking canes were photographed standing by the fishpond at the foot of the steps leading to the shelter. Smith transformed many other derelict or waste areas, constructing popular parks and gardens for both locals and visiting tourists to enjoy. His love of creating foreign themes led to the construction of Peasholm Park as an oriental garden in 1911, using local unemployed men as labourers. The land upon which Peasholm Park was built was formerly known as Tucker's Field. Today, the Borough Council continue to maintain over 2,000 acres of parks and woodland, with staff dedicated to care for all the flora, fauna and wildlife to be found there. Plants for the Italian and other gardens are cultivated at the Council's own nurseries.

The full extent of the Italian Gardens is captured in this old photograph looking south. It was taken in the days when dress was formal, even in casual circumstances. All of the women are wearing long flowing dresses and wide-brimmed hats. The ladies dressed in black are likely to be widowed, as the convention of the times was strictly adhered to up until the Second World War. Today's fashions are much less formal, though the style of the Italian Gardens remains pretty much as it was in earlier times. As can be seen from both photographs, the central fishpond with its classical statue has been a constant feature throughout the years.

This third set of pictures shows that in reality, though called the Italian Gardens, the area was actually originally laid out as a typical English park garden with rustic wooden fences, rose bushes and English trees, though no doubt the steps, classical statue and shelter with its columned supports were meant to imply a touch of the Mediterranean. In the lower and later of the two old views, palm trees and more luxurious shrubs had been added. Arches had also been built above the open entrances to the shelter and some sort of flowering creeper had been grown across its flat roof to give a more continental touch to the building. Glass windows and shutters, absent from the top view, can be seen on the end of the structure in the bottom one, no doubt to protect visitors from wind and rain in inclement weather. It is interesting to see that the palm tree featured in the lower of the old photographs is still in existence in the modern view today.

On the South Cliff, high above the Italian Gardens, other opportunities for leisure are offered. Though the year the old picture was taken is not known, the outfits worn by those playing on the putting green would appear to indicate some time in the late 1950s. The clock tower tells us that the time was 10.30 a.m. precisely, by which time many of those pictured would have just left their boarding houses or hotel rooms nearby on the South Cliff. The scene is little changed today and the clock tower still stands behind the putting green, often being featured in scenes from the television hospital series *The Royal*. The building used for the hospital scenes stands just outside the camera view to the left on Holbeck Road.

No doubt some of these refined and well-dressed holidaymakers on the Esplanade had just arrived at the top of the cliff using the spa tramway. They are carrying parasols (not umbrellas) to protect their complexions from what was considered the harsh seaside sunlight. Wide-brimmed hats were also worn for the same purpose. As one commentator of the time tells us: 'Life in Scarborough is a very sophisticated, not to say of a treadmill character. Everybody feeds at the same hours; everybody goes to the Spa at the proper times; most do a little fishing and a little flirting, and wind up at a concert or a dance'. The life of the ordinary people of the town at that time would of course been quite different, and away from the expensive areas frequented by the rich and famous, residents carried on their lives regardless. Today, visitors still walk along this area of the cliff, though often motor cars are now more numerous than visitors.

Long walks and playing on the putting green was and still is a feature of the leisure facilities to be found in Peasholm Park. The pagoda, damaged in recent times by a fire, is seen here dominating the scene at Peasholm Park created from land known as Tucker's Field in 1911. The park has incorporated a number of recreational features over the years, including winding lakeside walks through parks and gardens, miniature golf, boating, a suspended tree walk and a café. This old scene appears to have been taken in the 1920s or '30s and shows that the timeless pursuits such as boating and miniature golf were at that time as popular as they are today.

A stone's throw from previous scene stands Scarborough's outdoor swimming pool, one of the few major outdoor pools left in the country and possibly soon to be demolished. The pool, seen here in its heyday, was once one of Scarborough's major attractions, with visitors coming from far and wide to enjoy its attractions. Such was its popularity that Whitby schoolchildren would regularly travel the twenty-mile journey each weekend by bus in order to bathe in the pool, even though the town of Whitby had its own outdoor pool at that time. Peasholm Park, seen to the right of the picture, stands on the ancient manor of Northstead, the stewardship of which, like the Chiltern Hundreds, was applied for as part of the procedure for the resignation of Members of Parliament. Behind it is the main town of Scarborough, with Oliver's Mount in the distance. The modern picture, taken from the hill on the left shown in the old photograph, shows the closed pool as it stands today.

The changing face of the leisure facilities at the end of the North Bay centred for many years at what was affectionately known as the 'Corner Café'. Here cars and buses arrived, dropping off their passengers who then proceeded on foot to Peasholm Park, the swimming pool, the beach or one of the many other attractions in the same area. The scene opposite is taken from an old postcard which itself attempted to show how the scene had changed from the 1920s to the 1950s. At the time this updated modern picture was taken, workers were getting ready for the summer season and buses and cars were still dropping off and picking up their passengers at the same point, though today many of the facilities are being changed, demolished or re-planned in order to cater for the the more sophisticated tastes of the modern holidaymaker.

Change has been continuous over the years at Scarborough, as the taste of its visitors have changed. Just after the Second World War, Scarborough began to redevelop itself as a major 'modern' leisure resort. The North Bay became popular for the more 'discerning' of the town's visitors who wished to avoid the crowds who were disparagingly termed the 'candy-floss and lollypop brigade'. Family groups from all classes of society saw the North Bay as a quieter area of recreation and manual workers who had arrived by bus mixed easily with more wealthy holidaymakers who would demonstrate their wealth by arriving in their own vehicles, often driven by a chauffer. Though car ownership was not common in British society at that time, it is interesting to note the number of privately owned motor vehicles lined up along the roadside at the right of the old picture. In the distance can be seen the castle and below it an area known as 'Hairy Bob's hole', supposedly from a hole dug by a tramp who lived there.

The castle has always been a popular visitor attraction. As can be seen from these two photographs, it has changed little over the years, though the area around has been developed tremendously. In 1888 it was thought that roads skirting the South Bay and North Bay would never be joined unless a tunnel could be cut under the castle hill. It was written that: 'The eastern bluff of the Castle Rock is so steep and base, is so beset with huge stones, that there is no possibility of making a road or even a footpath round it. The two foreshores are therefore entirely cut off from one another'. Just twenty years later in 1908 the Marine Drive was officially opened after more than eight years' work.

The visitors strolling around the castle in December 1914 were to get quite a shock. This pair of pictures illustrates the scene in early December 1914 when the castle barracks were attacked from the sea without warning by German warships. It is not known if the old illustration is a photograph or a painting but it is known to accurately depict the event as it took place. The gravestone in the centre foreground is still in existence and as can be seen from the modern photograph taken from the same viewpoint in St Mary's churchyard, the amount of damage inflicted on the castle walls was quite substantial. In the centre of the modern picture, running from left to right, a new row of houses has replaced those in the old one, though the other row of houses with large chimneys running from the foreground into the distance remain much as they were in 1914.

The churchyard surrounding the parish church of St Mary has long been a place to wander in silence for those seeking quieter leisure pursuits. There has been a building here since a Roman signal station stood on the promontory around AD 370. It was once much larger in size, having three towers, a central one and two at the west end. The central tower eventually collapsed, causing great damage to the rest of the structure. The present tower was built in 1669 with restoration of the structure taking place during 1850 and 1890. The religious establishment started its life as a Cistercian chapel. For many years the ruins of the former establishment lay to the eastern side of it. In 1645 the Roundheads destroyed the chancel when they used it as headquarters during the Civil War. In this old print residents are examining the ancient gravestones and today many still visit to do the same. One of the notable gravestones in the present-day churchyard is that of Anne Brontë.

Two scenes here show the South Foreshore in December 1914 and in December 2004. The old illustration depicts the visitor attractions on the seafront which also took a direct hit from the German shells when the castle was hit. The Picture House (left of the old picture) was badly damaged. Despite much panic during the bombardment, some of the town's residents went on with their work regardless. A postman, Alfred Beal, lost his life while delivering mail, and a milkman named Leng who left his cart to deliver milk on Seamer Road returned just as a shell landed nearby, killing his horse instantly. The brave churchgoers at St Martin's church were in the middle of early morning Communion when shells started exploding. Ignoring the noises of masonry falling and glass shattering, they continued with their services until its conclusion. The lighthouse, castle walls and castle barracks were also hit, as was the town hospital which, though damaged, managed to carry on caring for the injured as they arrived for treatment.

A visitor bought stamps at Merryweather's corner shop just before the bombardment and wrote a postcard home saying, 'Dear Aggie. This is not the holiday of rest I expected. You may have heard about the shelling. I was there. If I had bought the stamp for this postcard 10 minutes later, I may never have seen you again...' The shop she was referring to was Joseph Merryweather's corner shop and post office (run by G.H. Merryweather) at Prospect Road. It was badly damaged by a shell aimed at the Falsgrave telegraph station. Other main targets were the town's gasworks and the waterworks. Mrs Merryweather ran out of the shop to invite neighbours to shelter in the shop cellar. As they returned the building was hit, gravely injuring Mrs Merryweather who died in a carriage on the way to the local doctor. Her friends and neighbours, though standing nearby, survived without serious injury. Today the building and the post box that probably contained the postcard mentioned earlier, are now gone forever.

It is interesting to note that the leisure interests of Scarborough residents have remained constant in their support of local football teams. This rare old photograph is said to show the cabs waiting for the crowds to leave Scarborough Athletic Ground. The horse-drawn covered bus in the scene is plastered with advertisements including those for Simpson's store and Cadbury's chocolate. Along the back of the bus roof is a large slogan: 'Zebra Grate Polish'. This product often came in the shape of a large tube, looking very much like black toothpaste. It was used in almost every household to blacken and polish the fire grate and metal fireplace fixtures. It is interesting to note that the bus driver and the cab men are all gaining a free view of the football match by standing on their vehicles and looking over the fence. Today's scene outside the football field is very different and few (except perhaps those living in houses nearby) have the privilege of watching Scarborough matches without paying the usual entrance fee.